RIVER
ADVENTURES

THAMES RIVER

A+
Smart Apple Media

Published by Smart Apple Media
P.O. Box 3263, Mankato, Minnesota 56002
www.smartapplemedia.com

Published by arrangement with the Watts Publishing
Group LTD, London.

Library of Congress Cataloging-in-Publication Data

Manning, Paul.
 The Thames River / Paul Manning.
    p. cm. -- (River adventures)
 Includes bibliographical references and index.
 Summary: "Follow the Thames River through the
beautiful English countryside as you learn about its
tributaries and the surrounding landscape. Discover
the culture and history of Oxford University, Windsor
Castle, and London from the Thames River"--Provided
by publisher.
 ISBN 978-1-59920-918-0 (library binding)
 1. Thames Valley (England)--Description and travel-
-Juvenile literature. 2. London (England)--History--
Juvenile literature. I. Title.
 DA670.T2M26 2015
 942.2--dc23
 2012035419

ISBN: 978-1-59920-918-0   (library binding)
ISBN: 978-1-62588-588-3   (eBook)

Design, editing, and picture research by Paul Manning
Maps by Stefan Chabluk

Printed in the United States by CG Book Printers
North Mankato, Minnesota

PO 1732
3-2015

9 8 7 6 5 4 3 2 1

Key to Images

Top cover image: The Thames Barrier at Woolwich
Main cover image: Tower Bridge, with HMS *Belfast*
in the foreground.
Previous page: A mother swan and cygnets
on the Thames.
This page: A panorama of the Thames
at Westminster.

Picture Credits

Main cover image, Shutterstock/DelicatePhoto; small cover image,
Wikimedia/Diliff; 1, Dreamstime/Cata37; 2, Shutterstock/crazychris84;
4, Dreamstime/Chris Lofty; 5a (map) Stefan Chabluk; 5b, Wikimedia/
Keven Law; 6, Wikimedia/Jo Sayers; 7a, Wikimedia/David McManamon;
7b, Wikimedia/Brian Robert Marshall; 8, Wikimedia/Andrew
Gray; 9a, Wikimedia/Jpbowen; 9b, Shutterstock/Tom Davison; 10,
Photolibrary/Jon Bower; 11a, Wikimedia/Motmit; 11b, Chris Morris; 12,
Shutterstock/Filip Fuxa; 13, Corbis/Ted Spiegel; 14, Wikimedia/Andreas
Praefcke; 15a,15b, courtesy Thames Water; 16, Photolibrary/Loop
Images/Mike Kirk; 17a, Shutterstock/AISPIX; 17b, Wikimedia Commons/
Mark Barker; 18, Wikimedia/Aurelien Guichard; 19a, Wikimedia/
Diliff; 19b, courtesy Transport for London; 20, Shutterstock/bajars;
21a, Shutterstock/CJPhoto; 21b, Wikimedia/Alex1011; 22, RichTea;
23, Arpingstone; 24, Dreamstime/Stormcab; 25a, Adrian Pingstone;
25b, Dreamstime/Jyothi; 26, Dreamstime/Mark6138; 27a, Wikimedia/
Andy Roberts; 27b, Dreamstime/Rsaraiva; 28, Wikimedia/Colin Park;
29a, Corbis/Richard Cummins; 31a, Dreamstime/Honourableandbold;
31b,Wikimedia/John Thaxter; 31c, Wikimedia/Convit; 31d, Wikimedia;
31e, Dreamstime/Marquarita; 31f, Dreamstime/Anthony Baggett; 31g,
Wikimedia/Udimu.

CONTENTS

A Thames Journey

The Thames River is famous for its history, scenery, and wildlife. It follows a winding **course** through southern England, flowing from the Cotswold hills east toward London and beyond. You will follow its 219-mile (352-km) journey from **source** to sea.

▼ The Thames is the longest river entirely in England and the second longest river in the United Kingdom. Before reaching London, it passes through several towns.

England's River

The Thames has shaped England's landscape since prehistoric times. In the first century bc, Roman London grew up on its banks. In the eighteenth and nineteenth centuries, ships traveled the river carrying raw materials from all over the British Empire. Many famous events took place on or near the Thames, and your journey will take you past many of England's best-known landmarks.

A Cleaner River

Sixty years ago, the Thames was so **polluted** that scientists thought it would never recover. In the 1960s, a big cleanup began, and fish once more began to appear in it. Now, it is one of the world's least polluted **urban** rivers.

Where is the source?

The Thames starts as a tiny spring bubbling out of the ground at Thames Head near the village of Kemble in Gloucestershire. Or does it? Some say it should be measured from a place called Severn Springs, which is near Andoversford, 11 miles (18 km) farther north. Severn Springs is the source of the Churn River, which joins the Thames at Cricklade.

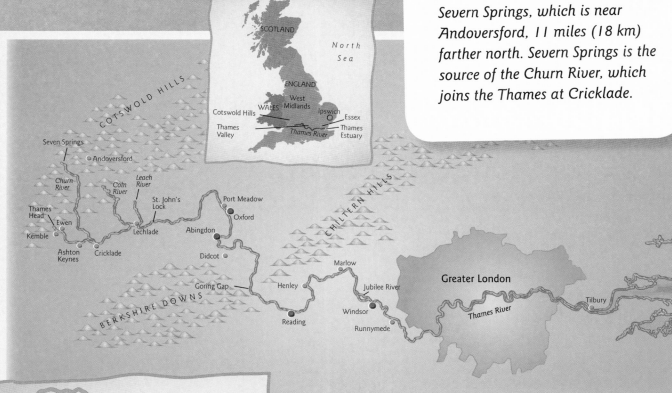

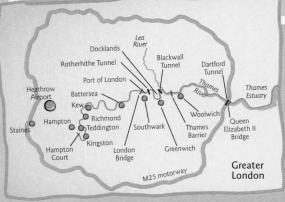

▶ Otters once disappeared from the Thames, but they are slowly returning as the river becomes cleaner.

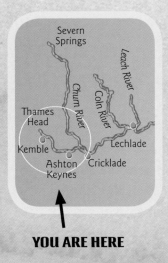

Severn
Springs

Leach River

Churn River

Coln River

Thames
Head

Kemble

Lechlade

Ashton
Keynes

Cricklade

YOU ARE HERE

The Cotswolds

For the first part of its journey, the Thames is little more than a stream flowing through the Cotswold countryside. At this point, the river is too shallow for boats, so you have to follow the route on foot.

Soon after leaving Kemble, you pass the pretty Cotswold village of Ashton Keynes. Many of the cottages are reached by their own tiny, stone bridge across the river. The water is crystal clear, and you can see schools of tiny fish darting among the weeds.

▼ *This shady stretch of the river is a perfect place to fish for* **minnows.**

Thames Tributaries

On its journey, the Thames is joined by many smaller streams called **tributaries**, which add to its flow. Near Cricklade, it is joined by the Churn. A little farther on at Lechlade, the Leach and Coln flow into it too, and the water becomes deep enough for boats. The Thames has 50 tributaries, not including canals.

▲ In earlier times, Lechlade, just beyond this lock, was the highest point on the river that could be reached by barge.

In the Middle Ages, barges traveled from Lechlade, carrying goods to market in London. Mills along the river used water power to grind corn.

▶ These rare wild flowers are called snake's head fritillaries. They are only found in flood meadows beside the Thames.

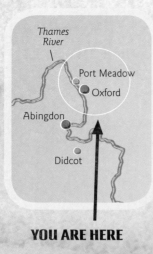

YOU ARE HERE

The Isis

At Oxford, the Thames is called the Isis from its Latin name *Tame-isis*. Oxford gets its name from the words "oxen **ford**," which is the place where oxen cross (ford) the river.

Port Meadow

As you approach the city, a huge field known as Port Meadow opens out on your left. In the winter, the meadow is often covered in water and freezes to form a natural ice rink. Low-lying fields like this are very important for absorbing floodwater from the river and as a wildlife habitat. Many meadows are disappearing as land is used for farming or for housing.

▼ Folly Bridge, south of the city, is Oxford's oldest river crossing. Cattle forded the Thames here in ancient times.

◄ The river at Oxford is widely used for sport, leisure, and recreation.

Sports on the River

Rowing has been popular in Oxford since the eighteenth century when college crews called "eights" first started to hold races on the river. Today, the big event is the University Boat Race. It is held between Putney and Mortlake in London each year when Oxford takes on its archrival, Cambridge.

A University Town

Closer to the city center, you can see a cluster of spires, domes, and old buildings. Many have fine lawns and gardens stretching down to the river. These are the colleges of Oxford University.

Oxford has been a university town since the thirteenth century, when religious **scholars** founded the first colleges. Oxford is ranked among the top 10 universities in the world. Huge numbers of tourists come to Oxford to visit the university and its buildings.

► Riverside walks and fine buildings like the Radcliffe Camera (built as a library) attract many visitors to Oxford.

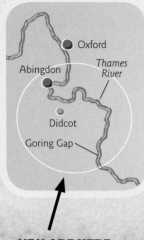

YOU ARE HERE

The Thames Valley

Beyond Oxford, the Thames winds through gently rolling countryside. The land is very **fertile** and has supported human life for thousands of years.

▼ *Abingdon, south of Oxford, is one of Britain's oldest towns. There has been a* **settlement** *here for at least 6,000 years.*

Natural Resources

In prehistoric times, the Thames Valley was a good place to live. People grew crops and grazed their cattle by the river. As well as freshwater, the Thames provided fish to eat and a wide range of natural resources. These included reeds, rushes, and timber for building. The riverbed was also full of flint, which was useful for making sharp tools such as axes.

◄ At the Goring Gap, the Thames heads south between the Chiltern Hills and the Berkshire Downs.

The Goring Gap

At Goring, near Reading, the sides of the valley become steeper. The landscape has been dramatically shaped by the river.

Originally, the Thames followed a northeasterly route, rising in the West Midlands and flowing through Hertfordshire and Essex into the North Sea near Ipswich. After the last **Ice Age**, torrents of water from melting glaciers forced the river to change course. Instead of flowing northeast, the Thames carved its way south, creating the **gorge** called the Goring Gap.

Soil Erosion

As a river flows, the force of its moving water washes away loose soil and rock. In this way, the river cuts its own channel in the ground. The process of wearing away rocks is called **erosion**. *With a slow-moving river such as the Thames, erosion can take place gradually over thousands of years.*

► Eel, salmon, and trout have been caught in the Thames since ancient times. These anglers have landed a pike.

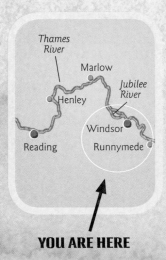

YOU ARE HERE

A Royal River

After Reading, the Thames heads north to Henley before turning east and south again toward Marlow. Continuing downriver, Windsor Castle comes into view.

A Defensive Site

Windsor Castle began as a wooden fort built at the time of the **Norman Conquest**. William the Conqueror chose the site because it overlooked the river and was easy to defend. As the castle grew, the town of Windsor grew up around it. Today, the castle is one of the main homes of the British royal family, and a popular tourist site.

▼ The river is a natural barrier protecting the castle at Windsor.

The Jubilee River

Windsor Castle is well protected on its high mound, but the land around it has often been affected by floods. In 1947, the river rose to approximately 6.5 feet (2 m) higher than usual. Large areas were flooded, and many people were trapped in their homes. In 2001, the Jubilee River channel was created to protect the region from flooding.

Runnymede

Shortly after Windsor, you pass the **water meadow** of Runnymede. A small island on the north bank is believed to be where King John signed the Magna Carta in 1215. This "great charter" was the first successful attempt to limit the power of the king and protect the rights of English people. Runnymede means "a meeting place in the meadow."

▶ Boatmen carry out the annual task of counting swans on the Thames near Windsor. Each swan is checked for disease and injury before being placed back in the water.

Greater London

As you approach London, the landscape changes. Jets fly overhead, bound for Heathrow Airport, and the river passes under the M25, London's busy highway.

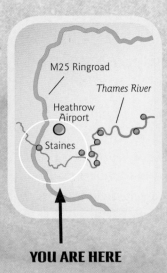

YOU ARE HERE

▼ These lakes and reservoirs on the outskirts of London store water from the Thames.

The Commuter Belt

On this part of your journey, you pass through some of the most densely populated parts of the United Kingdom. More than 8 million people live in Greater London. Many businesses are located here because of its transport and communications links. This is also the city's "**commuter** belt," where people live and travel to work in central London.

◀ At this treatment plant, **wastewater** from homes and factories is **decontaminated** before being fed back into the river.

Who needs water?

About 79 percent of London's water is used in people's homes. The rest is used by industries, including breweries and paper-makers. Some of the biggest users are power stations like the one at Didcot in Berkshire where Thames water is used to cool the giant electricity **turbines**.

Lakes and Reservoirs

At Staines, the Thames heads south, crisscrossing under roads and highways and weaving among lakes and reservoirs.

As well as being a place for recreation and a transport route, the river is a vital source of water for London. Every day, millions of gallons of water from the Thames are diverted to lakes and reservoirs. Water is then pumped to treatment works to be cleaned and filtered before being piped to people's homes.

▶ At a Thames Water laboratory, a scientist examines a water sample to make sure it is clean and safe to drink.

The Tidal Thames

Thames
River

Kew

Richmond

Hampton

Teddington

Hampton
Court

Kingston

YOU ARE HERE

▼ *Teddington Weir marks the start of the tidal section of the Thames, known as the* **tideway**.

At Teddington Lock, you reach an important stage in your journey. Here, freshwater meets saltwater carried in from the sea. From now on, the Thames is a tidal river.

The Tide Effect

Although the sea is nearly 65 miles (105 km) away, the tide has a big effect on the river. Instead of flowing steadily out toward the sea, the fresh water heading downstream is pushed back by the incoming tide. Depending on the strength of the tide, the water that flows over Teddington Weir can take from three weeks to three months to reach the sea.

▶ Hampton Court was well connected to London by river. Over the palace gate, a clock still shows the time of high tide at London Bridge.

Parks and Palaces

Between Hampton and Kew, the river is famous for its stately homes and royal parks and palaces. Many of these sites were chosen because of their riverside location.

Hampton Court was the favorite palace of Henry VIII. Kings, queens, and important people often traveled this stretch of the river in royal barges. Traveling with the tide made the journey much quicker, so trips up and down the river were carefully timed.

Controlling the Tide

At Richmond, a very low tide could mean that the river was little more than a shallow stream. Under this bridge, a **barrage** has been built with gates, which can be raised and lowered. This protects boats moored upstream from running aground when the tide goes out.

◀ The barrage at Richmond helps to control the effect of the tide.

The Working River

Past the green spaces of Richmond and Kew, you are now in urban West London. Here, the river is lined with offices, apartments, warehouses, and industrial buildings.

Thames
River

Battersea

Kew

YOU ARE HERE

▼ *Battersea Power Station once produced electricity for the whole of London, but it has not been used since 1982. Coal was brought by river every day and unloaded by cranes that still stand on the waterfront.*

A Transport Route

In the past, the river was a vital transport route. Many industries were based along its banks. The ships and barges carried supplies of coal and other raw materials that were unloaded at **wharves** on the waterfront.

◀ Barges towed by tugboats were once a common sight on the river. Today, most heavy goods are carried by road or rail.

As London grew, road and rail transport gradually took over from the boats and use of the river **declined**. Today, a few working boats can be seen, but most of the traffic on the river is made up of tourist or pleasure boats.

Bridges and Tunnels

Until the eighteenth century, London Bridge was the only place in London where the river could be crossed. Today, there are 33 bridges across the Thames between Hampton and Southwark. **Pedestrian** and rail tunnels have also been built underneath the Thames. Road tunnels have been built at Blackwall, Rotherhithe, and Dartford.

Commuting by River

Riverbus is a good way to travel this stretch of the Thames. There are no traffic jams, and you can enjoy some of the best views of London from the river. More than 2,000 commuters a day travel to work on the Thames. Catching a riverbus is as easy as catching a bus or underground train.

Westminster

Thames River

Westminster

Battersea

YOU ARE HERE

At Westminster, your boat ride takes you past some of London's most historic buildings. Since 1066, 38 English kings and queens have been crowned in Westminster Abbey. Laws have been debated in the houses of Parliament since the thirteenth century.

▼ The Houses of Parliament overlook the Thames at Westminster.

► *The Millennium footbridge connects the South Bank with St. Paul's Cathedral. It is the newest bridge over the Thames.*

The Embankment

The Thames flows between high stone walls called **embankments**. These were built beginning in 1862 in Queen Victoria's reign to protect the city from flooding. Before this, the river was flanked by muddy land. Much of London's sewage ended up here, and many Londoners died from diseases caused by drinking water from the river.

The London Eye

On the north bank, the Victoria Embankment carries a steady stream of traffic east and west through the city. The giant ferris wheel known as the London Eye is on the other side of the river. From the top of this, you have a far-reaching view of the Thames as it flows through London.

► *London's embankments and sewers were designed by Joseph Bazalgette (1819–91). His memorial stands on the Victoria Embankment.*

The "Great Stink"

During a heat wave in 1858, the smell of sewage in the Thames was so bad that Parliament had to be **suspended**. *Afterward, the government decided to build a huge, new system of tunnels to get rid of the city's waste. The new sewers stopped drinking water from being contaminated by sewage. This saved the lives of thousands of Londoners.*

FLVM'N' · VINC'LA · P°SV'T

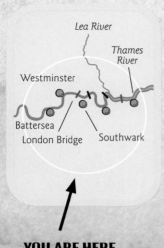

Lea River

Thames River

Westminster

Battersea

London Bridge

Southwark

YOU ARE HERE

▼ *The earliest crossing at London Bridge was built of wood. The present stone bridge dates from 1973. It leads directly to the London financial district.*

The Port of London

A river crossing has existed on the site of London Bridge since Roman times. It was here that London began, as a tiny settlement on the banks of the Thames.

An Ancient Crossing

The first bridge over the Thames was built by the Romans in around 50 bc. The Romans chose the site carefully: it was the farthest point inland where seagoing ships could anchor in the tidal waters of the Thames. On the river banks, a port was built where goods could be unloaded. The Roman town of Londinium grew up around it.

▲ Tower Bridge at the entrance to the old Port of London has sections of road called bascules. These can be raised to let tall ships through.

River Trade

The river has brought wealth to London ever since. In the eighteenth and nineteenth centuries, London was the busiest port in the world. There were so many vessels on the Thames, it was said that you could cross the river by stepping from one ship to the next!

The Growth of the Docks

The original Port of London was based between London Bridge and Wapping. As trade increased, shipping companies built their own docks farther downstream. The last to be built was the King George V dock in 1921.

The Thames Tunnel

The Thames Tunnel at Rotherhithe was the world's first underwater tunnel. It was built by the engineer Isambard Kingdom Brunel and his father Mark Isambard Brunel between 1825 and 1843. Digging under the riverbed was highly dangerous. Floods often occurred when the roof collapsed, and mud and water poured in.

Docklands

As you head east from Tower Bridge, you can see a cluster of high-rise blocks ahead of you. These are the giant towers of London's Docklands.

Lea River

Rotherhithe Tunnel

Blackwall Tunnel

Westminster

Greenwich

Docklands

Thames River

YOU ARE HERE

▼ *The business and financial district at Canary Wharf is the heart of modern Docklands. Around 90,000 people work here.*

The End of the Docks

Over the last 30 years, this area has changed. In the 1960s, the London docks began to close down one by one as trade shifted to bigger ports near the sea. Within a few years, the docks had become a **derelict** wasteland.

In the 1980s, a huge building project transformed the old warehouses and wharves into new riverside communities. Smart new flats and offices were built around the dock basins. By 1998, more than 24,000 new homes had been built, and 2,700 new businesses had moved into the area.

A Naval Town

At Greenwich, you visit the National Maritime Museum. The famous Harrison Clocks that first allowed sailors to plot their position accurately on long sea voyages are on display. Greenwich is also the home of the *Cutty Sark*, a great, tall-masted sailing ship that once raced to bring back cargoes of tea from China.

Policing the Thames

Since 1800, fighting crimes on the river has been the job of the Thames River Police. In the past, smuggling was common, and cargo ships on the Thames were often a target for river pirates. Today, police launches are more likely to be on the lookout for drug runners and people traffickers.

▶ *Tourist boats and riverbuses bring visitors to the old Royal Naval College at Greenwich.*

The Thames Barrier

Around the site of the O2 Arena at Greenwich, the river turns a tight loop. Ahead of you are the giant piers of the Thames Barrier.

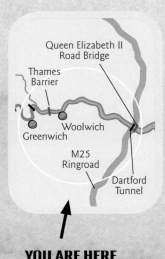

YOU ARE HERE

▼ *East of London, the low-lying landscape is flat. Many industries are based here. This part of the river was once heavily polluted by chemicals and other waste.*

The Thames Barrier

The Thames Barrier has been in place since 1984. It is London's main defense against flooding. Between the piers, huge curved gates are below the water. Normally, the gates are lowered to allow ships to pass through. When the flood risk is high, the gates are raised to hold back the tide.

The Thames Barrier is only part of London's flood defenses. There are 36 other, smaller barriers, and more than 115 miles (185 km) of defense walls along the riverbanks. On average, the Thames Barrier closes three times a year to protect London from surge tides from the sea. Luckily, no high storm tides are forecast today, so you can continue safely on your way.

What is a surge tide?

When storms at sea coincide with high tides, a surge tide can sweep upriver, causing flooding and widespread destruction. London is at risk because much of the land on which it is built is low-lying. Experts say the city is sinking at a rate of 12 inches (30 cm) every 100 years.

▶ The Queen Elizabeth II road bridge crosses the river at Dartford. The height of the bridge allows cruise ships to pass under it on their way to the Port of London.

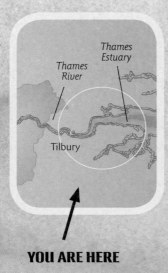

YOU ARE HERE

The Thames Estuary

As the Thames flows toward the sea, it opens out into a broad expanse of mudflats and **salt marshes**. Your river journey is nearly over.

A Shipping Route

This part of the Thames is a busy route for oil tankers, **container ships**, bulk carriers, and ferries. The river is wide and moves slowly at this point. Parts of it are flanked by wide banks called levees, which protect the land on either side from flooding.

▼ Egypt Bay on the Thames Estuary was once a favorite spot for smugglers bringing stolen goods ashore.

Tilbury

In ancient times, Tilbury was important in defending the river from enemy ships and preventing attacks on London. Today, Tilbury Docks is one of the busiest ports in the United Kingdom, handling passenger ships and container vessels from all over the world.

▲ *A container ship heads up the estuary toward Tilbury Docks.*

The Future

As London continues to grow, the future of the Thames Estuary is uncertain. With the completion of the high-speed Channel Tunnel Rail Link, the region is set to become a center for new jobs and housing. London's fourth airport may be located here too.

New development will certainly bring wealth, but many are concerned about the impact on wildlife, especially the many wading birds that live in the area.

Thames Barges

Thames barges were perfect for sailing the shallow waters of the Thames Estuary. Restored barges still sail the river today. Built of wood with huge sails, the barges were originally used to transport bricks, sand, coal, and grain. Over time, they were gradually replaced by steam-powered vessels.

Glossary

barrage a barrier to halt or reduce the flow of a river

commuter a person who travels to work by car, bus, or train

container ship a ship that transports goods in steel crates

course the route followed by a river

decline to reduce or become less

decontaminate to clean or remove impurities

derelict abandoned and run-down

embankment a high wall used to contain the flow of a river

erosion the gradual wearing away of soil or rock

fertile good for growing

ford a place where a river is shallow and can be crossed; also, to cross a shallow river

gorge a deep river valley with steep rocky sides

Ice Age a time long ago when the temperature dropped and Earth was covered with ice

lock a device for lifting or lowering boats from one level of water to another

minnow a tiny fish that lives in shallow water

Norman Conquest the time from 1066 onward when Britain was conquered by the Normans

pedestrian a person who travels on foot

polluted made dirty or contaminated, e.g., by sewage

reservoir a lake used to store water

salt marsh an area of muddy land in a coastal area

scholar a person who spends their time studying

settlement a place where people live permanently

source the beginning of a river, usually a lake or spring

suspended canceled or abandoned

tideway the part of a river that is affected by tides

tributary a stream or river that flows into another, bigger one

turbine a wheel that is turned by water to produce electricity

urban belonging to a town or city

wastewater water that has been washed down a drain

water meadow a field that is partly flooded at certain times of year

weir a type of dam used to control the flow of a river

wharf (*pl.* **wharves**) a place beside a river where goods are unloaded

Thames Quiz

Look up information in this book or online. Find the answers on page 32.

1 Match the captions to the pictures.

1

2

3

4

5

6

A   *The London Eye*

B   *A pier of the Thames Barrier at Woolwich*

C   *The statue of the Sphinx on the Victoria Embankment*

D   *A deer in Windsor Great Park*

E   *Boating on the river at Oxford*

F   *The statue of Old Father Thames at Lechlade Lock*

2 These places can all be found along the Thames. Put them in the right order, starting with the ones nearest to the sea:

Windsor
Hampton Court
Tilbury Docks
Abingdon
Lechlade
Battersea

3 True or false?

The Thames was once a tributary of the Rhine River that flows through Germany.

4 This bronze head is on display in the British Museum. Do you know who it represents and where it was found?

Websites and Further Reading

Websites

- *www.museumoflondon.org.uk/Explore-online/Pocket-histories*
  Interesting information about the early history of the river.

- *www.riverthames.co.uk/about-thames-information*
  A great source of facts and history about the Thames.

Further Reading

Green, Jen. *Rivers Around the World* (Geography Now). PowerKids Press, 2009.

Lister, Maree, Marit Sevier and Roseline Ngcheong-Lum. *England* (Welcome to my Country). Marshall Cavendish Benchmark, 2011.

Index

Answers to Thames Quiz
1 1D, 2F, 3C, 4E, 5A, 6B. **2** Tilbury Docks, Battersea, Hampton Court, Windsor, Abingdon, Lechlade. **3** True. Before Britain was separated from continental Europe, the two rivers met in the area now covered by southern North Sea. **4** The bronze head is part of a statue of the Roman Emperor Hadrian. It was found buried in the mud below London Bridge in 1834.